STAGECOACH
BEYOND SCOTLAND

THE FIRST TWENTY YEARS

STAGECOACH BEYOND SCOTLAND

THE FIRST TWENTY YEARS

KEITH A. JENKINSON

AMBERLEY

First published 2019

Amberley Publishing
The Hill, Stroud
Gloucestershire, GL5 4EP

www.amberley-books.com

Copyright © Keith A. Jenkinson, 2019

The right of Keith A. Jenkinson to be identified
as the Author of this work has been asserted in
accordance with the Copyrights, Designs and
Patents Act 1988.

ISBN 978 1 4456 8487 1 (print)
ISBN 978 1 4456 8488 8 (ebook)

British Library Cataloguing in Publication Data.
A catalogue record for this book is available from
the British Library.

Origination by Amberley Publishing.
Printed in the UK.

Introduction

After establishing itself in Scotland, Stagecoach gained its first foothold south of the border on 4 April 1987 when, through its newly formed holding company Skipburn Ltd (whose directors were Ann Gloag, Brian Souter, their uncle Frazer McColl and Hampshire Bus Managing Director Dawson Williams), it purchased the 216-vehicle Hampshire Bus and its associated Pilgrim Coaches from the National Bus Company. Almost before the ink had dried, on 26 April Pilgrim Coaches was closed down, with its fleet and operations being transferred to the parent company. Soon afterwards, the new owners of Hampshire Bus sold its Southampton premises at Grosvenor Square and Bedford Place, together with Southampton bus station, for redevelopment.

Seeking further expansion, Stagecoach, through its holding company Skipburn Ltd, made a successful offer for another National Bus Company subsidiary, Cumberland Motor Services, taking control on 23 July 1987. This, it was claimed, made Stagecoach the largest independent bus company in Western Europe, with 560 vehicles, 1,400 staff and a group turnover in excess of £24 million. Meanwhile, to enhance its fleets, Hampshire Bus purchased ten Van Hool-McArdle-bodied Ailsa B55 double-deckers from South Yorkshire PTE, while in November Cumberland reintroduced crew operation in Carlisle with eight former London Routemasters, all but two of which had previously operated with Kelvin Scottish.

Surprisingly, on 3 October Hampshire Bus sold its Southampton operations together with eighty-two vehicles to Musterphantom Ltd, who traded as Solent Blue Line, while a month later, on 19 November, Stagecoach expanded again when it purchased United Counties Omnibus Co. from the National Bus Company, adding another 249 buses and coaches to its growing empire.

1988 proved to be a year during which Stagecoach took stock of its new English subsidiaries, tweaking them where necessary, and consolidating its position in Cumbria with the purchase of independent operators Yeowarts of Whitehaven and Kirkpatrick of Brigham in May, as well as the bus operations of Brownriggs, Egremont, on 21 September. Meanwhile, although Stagecoach's three former NBC subsidiaries retained their independence and fleet names, a start was made in repainting their vehicles into the group's corporate striped livery. In addition, Stagecoach embarked upon its first overseas venture when it purchased a share in Hong Kong-based Speedybus Enterprises, a company that leased second-hand double-deckers to operators in China but did not operate any itself.

Following this, Stagecoach undertook another overseas venture when on 31 March 1989 it purchased United Transport International's 51 per cent share in United Transport Malawi Ltd. Almost immediately it changed its name to UTM and introduced double-deck buses to the fleet, with a Bristol Lodekka from Stagecoach Scotland and twelve Daimler CVG6LXs from Hong Kong-based Kowloon Motor Bus, from whom a further twenty-six were acquired in 1990. Meanwhile, back in the UK, Stagecoach continued to expand with its acquisition of East Midland Motor Services and its subsidiaries Rainworth Travel, Front Runner South East and Frontrunner North West on 7 April, Ribble Motor Services on 21 April, Stephenson of Maryport on 2 May, Barrow Borough Transport on 26 May, Southdown Motor Services on 16 August, Worthing-based Cedarbus on 25 September, Portsmouth Citybus on 20 October, Mercer of Longridge on 26 November, Palmer of Carlisle on 1 December, and eight days later, the Formia Group, who owned Hastings & District Transport and its subsidiary Eastbourne & District Transport. Included in the Southdown deal was its 51 per cent share in Hastings Top Line Buses, whose remaining 49 per cent, owned by Eastbourne Buses, was quickly acquired to give Stagecoach complete control. In a move to consolidate its operations, on 30 June Stagecoach sold its Frontrunner South East services to Ensignbus, Purfleet, following this on 30 September with its sale of Frontrunner North West to Drawlane. Both the Frontrunner operations had been started by East Midlands when, following deregulation in its pre-Stagecoach days, it had spread its wings to north London and Greater Manchester. Also on 30 September it sold its Ribble Bee Line minibus operation and most of its own Manchester operations to Drawlane. Then, looking to increase patronage, towards the end of the year United Counties introduced crew operation to some local services in Corby and Bedford using former London Routemasters, as well as relaunching its Street Shuttle minibus operations in Corby under the Magic Minis banner with a black and gold livery.

Continuing its acquisition trail, on 2 February 1990 Stagecoach, through its East Midlands subsidiary, purchased a 50 per cent stake in important independent Maun of Mansfield, acquiring the remaining 50 per cent on 7 April to give it complete control. Then, on 11 November, through its Cumberland subsidiary, it bought the competing small business of Cleator Moor-based Andy Vine. More surprising, however, was the purchase in June of Gray Coach Lines from its municipal owner Toronto Transit Commission, giving it its first foothold in Canada. In addition to operating express coach services it also maintained a sightseeing tour to Niagara Falls and, to test the waters in the operation of this with double-deckers, converted one of its UK Bristol FLF Lodekkas to open-top configuration, exporting it in early 1991.

1991 was largely a year of consolidation. No further acquisitions were made and concentration was given to fleet upgrading, with more new Alexander-bodied Leyland Olympians joining the combined fleet. However, upon the instruction of the Monopolies & Mergers Commission, who had been investigating Stagecoach's 1989 purchase of Portsmouth Citybus, the company was sold on 18 January together with

104 buses to Transit Holdings, who renamed it Portsmouth Transit. Also sold were Gray Coach Lines' northern routes, which passed to Ontario Northland Transportation Commission in April. Towards the end of the year, on 11 November Stagecoach moved into Africa again when it purchased United Transport Overseas Services' 75 per cent stake in Kenya Bus Services, who operated in both Nairobi and Mombasa with a total of 280 single-deck buses.

1992 proved to be eventful, with Stagecoach expanding its global reach, dipping its toe into railways, and continuing its expansion in the UK. Before this, however, on 2 April, it introduced changes to its south coast operations when it renamed Southdown Motor Services Ltd as Sussex Coastline Buses Ltd and Hastings & District Transport Ltd as South Coast Buses Ltd. Prior to this, on 23 March, Stagecoach Rail was born following a deal being struck with state-owned InterCity, which allowed it 116 seats on the overnight rail service from London Euston to Edinburgh and Aberdeen. Using six railway carriages leased from British Rail and painted in Stagecoach livery, the new service began on 11 May, but finding it less than successful, it was discontinued in October. As one door closed, however, others opened and on 25 October Stagecoach acquired Alder Valley (with the exception of its Londonlink express coach operation) from Len Wright's Q Drive group and immediately renamed it Stagecoach Hants & Surrey. Then, three days later it spread its wings across the globe to New Zealand, where it purchased the majority shareholding in Wellington City Transport, whose fleet comprised 228 vehicles, of which sixty-eight were trolleybuses, thus giving Stagecoach its first taste of electric propulsion. Sadly, however, its venture into Canada came to an end in December when, due to political interference, it sold its Gray Coach Lines operation and fleet to Greyhound Lines.

Still consolidating its operations, and at the same time continuing to seek expansion, on 27 April Stagecoach Holdings was floated on the London Stock Exchange when 33,505.954 ordinary shares were placed on offer with an initial share price of 112p. Then, three days later, Stagecoach East Midland sold its Midland Travel coaching unit, together with seven coaches, to Skill's of Nottingham to allow it to give greater concentration to its local bus operations. As a result of its increased competition in and around Morecambe, the local municipal operator, City of Lancaster Transport reluctantly ceased trading on 22 August and sold its depot and twenty-one buses to Stagecoach. Meanwhile, on 17 July, Stagecoach had sold its 50 per cent share in Hong Kong bus dealer Speedybus to its partner, Clement Lau. Moving forward to the autumn, on 7 September Stagecoach purchased East Kent Road Car Company, adding a further 243 buses to its UK portfolio. Stagecoach then followed this with the acquisition of municipally owned Grimsby Cleethorpes Transport and its Peter Sheffield coaching subsidiary on 18 November. Finally, on 10 December Stagecoach purchased the Western Travel Group, whose portfolio included Cheltenham District, City of Gloucester, Stroud Valleys, Swindon & District, Red & White, Midland Red South, G&G Travel, Vanguard and a 45 per cent stake in Gloucester independent Circle Line.

January 1994 began with Stagecoach returning to Hong Kong, this time as an operator rather than in conjunction with dealer Speedybus Enterprises, when on the 24th it launched two new 'Residents' routes upon which it operated five new

Alexander PS-bodied Volvo B10Ms fitted with air conditioning. Five days later it entered the Manchester arena when, in competition with GM Buses South, it began a service between the city centre, Stockport and Hazel Grove, upon which it used sixteen new Alexander-bodied Volvo B6s from a new depot at Bredbury. This was small fry, however, as on 26 July Stagecoach acquired 590-vehicle Tyne & Wear Busways (a company once owned by the PTE) together with its low-cost subsidiaries Blue Bus Service, Economic, Favourite and its Armstrong Galley coaching arm to give it a strong presence in north-east England. During the following month, in a bid to get a foothold in Sheffield, it purchased a 20 per cent share in the former South Yorkshire PTE Mainline Group before acquiring the remaining 55 per cent of Circle Line, Gloucester. With further expansion firmly on the cards, on 6 September Stagecoach moved south with its acquisition of two former London Buses subsidiaries – 590-bus East London Bus & Coach Company and 414-vehicle South East London & Kent Bus Company. One of the purchase stipulations was that its London fleet should retain a largely red livery and thus Stagecoach was not able to introduce its familiar corporate colours into the capital's central area. Moving back to the North East, in November Stagecoach strengthened its position when it bought Cleveland Transit together with its 51 per cent share in Kingston-upon-Hull City Transport, the remaining 49 per cent of which it purchased soon afterwards on the 14th of that month. In the meantime, after failing in its attempt to acquire Darlington Transport, Stagecoach launched an attack on the company on 7 November with fifty-four buses and a range of services upon which no fares were charged, forcing the municipal undertaking to cease trading four days later. Finally, Stagecoach purchased the employee-owned, former municipal, sixty-seven-bus Hartlepool Transport on 12 December, thus concluding an extremely eventful year.

After a quiet start to the new year, Stagecoach expanded its operations in New Zealand when, in June 1995, it acquired Runcimans Motors, which it incorporated into Cityline Hutt Valley. Then, during the same month, it acquired Tyneside independent Jolly of South Hylton following the retirement of its owner. On this occasion, however, no vehicles were included in the deal. Continuing its programme of expansion, on 27 July Chesterfield Transport, together with its subsidiaries Retford & District and coach operating company Whites of Calver, was acquired to add a further 112 vehicles to its ever-growing portfolio. Whites' coaching operation was immediately offered for sale, but after failing to find a buyer it was closed down in September. Further signalling its disinterest in coaching, Stagecoach Transit passed its Cleveland Coaches activities to Stockton independent Delta Coaches in exchange for its local bus operations, while on 2 September Stagecoach Midland Red South acquired the twelve-vehicle business of Oxhill-based David Grasby Coach Hire. In order to pave the way for the hopeful future purchase of GM Buses South, on 13 October Stagecoach sold its small Bredbury-based Manchester operation to EYMS-owned Finglands together with thirteen Alexander PS-bodied Volvo B10Ms. Then, just before the year ended, on 6 December Stagecoach purchased Cambus together with its subsidiaries Viscount Buses, Peterborough Bus Company, MK Metro, MK Citybus and Premier Travel Services.

Following an agreement reached with Montagu Private Equity to purchase a 25 per cent share in Rodoviária de Lisboa, who operated buses in Estoril, Cascais and

Lisbon and the small historic tramway in Sintra, Stagecoach began its new Portuguese operations on 1 January 1996. On the same day Stagecoach sold its 20 per cent share in Mainline to FirstBus, who had emerged as the successful bidder for the large South Yorkshire company. Undeterred, however, Stagecoach achieved another of its goals when it returned to railway operations, and on 4 February began its seven-year franchise to run South West Trains from London Waterloo to the south coast, Devon and Cornwall, thus becoming the first privatised scheduled train operator for forty-eight years. Following this, on 19 February, Stagecoach added bus operations to its new South West area when it purchased Transit Holdings Exeter-based Devon General and Torquay-based Bayline, who jointly operated 311 buses and were quickly merged under the title Stagecoach Devon. Then, proving to be a month of major expansion, eight days later Stagecoach acquired GM Buses South and its Charterplan coaching subsidiary to give it a major presence in Manchester, adding a further 744 buses to its UK fleet. As if this was not enough, in April Stagecoach purchased Pendle Council's 50 per cent share in Burnley & Pendle Transport, but failed to persuade its other shareholder, Burnley Borough Council, to sell its stake, and thus had to operate with it in a partnership. On the other side of the coin, on 31 March Stagecoach sold its small Hong Kong Resident's operation to Kwoon Chung Motors and its six Leyland Olympians to Hong Kong Citybus, while its five Volvo B10Bs were transferred to its New Zealand Citybus subsidiary. Then, looking perhaps to the future, on 11 June Stagecoach Cambus introduced two new CNG-powered Optare MetroRiders into Cambridge, where they were used on the free city centre shuttle. Later in the year, on 11 September, Stagecoach purchased municipal Hyndburn Borough Transport, thus adding a further sixty-five buses to its fleet and further consolidating its position in Lancashire. Continuing its search for expansion in mainland Europe, in October Stagecoach bought Swebus AB, the bus operating arm of the Swedish State Railways, together with its operations in Denmark, Finland and Norway. Meanwhile, back in the UK, Stagecoach purchased railway rolling stock-leasing company Porterbrook, and during this same month it began operating the Isle of Wight's railway, which connected Ryde Pier Head to Shanklin. This franchise differed from that of South West Trains, however, as it included maintenance of the track, stations and trains, the latter of which were former London Underground units.

1997 began with Stagecoach Busways selling its Armstrong Galley coaching business and sixteen coaches to East Yorkshire Travel on 4 January, while later in the month Stagecoach Red & White took over the Merthyr Tydfil to Brecon and Brecon to Swansea local bus services of Silverline, although no vehicles were involved in the deal. Following this and continuing to reduce its coaching operations, Stagecoach Hull sold its Kingstonian Travel arm and eight coaches to the EYMS Group, while on 8 March, to further consolidate its position in East Lancashire, Stagecoach purchased Burnley Borough Council's 50 per cent share in Burnley & Pendle Transport to give it total control of the company. Following this, to counter competition from independent HMB Buses in Newcastle-upon-Tyne, in April Stagecoach Busways launched three new low-cost routes using twenty-six of its older Leyland Atlanteans, which it repainted all-over blue and added Magic Bus branding to. At the beginning of April, Hull,

Darlington and Hartlepool were placed under Stagecoach Transit control to further consolidate its operations, and on the 26th of the month Hyndburn Transport ceased to exist as a separate company and was put under Ribble management, while its Manchester coaching operation, Charterplan, was sold to EYMS-owned Finglands. Then, on 2 May, after the long-awaited divestment of MK Metro following the MMC's ruling, it, along with 132 buses and United Counties' Huntingdon operations and depot, was sold to Premier Buses – a new company set up by Julian Peddle. Another departure from Stagecoach's portfolio was its complete withdrawal from Norway, following its failure to acquire a franchised operation in Oslo, when on 30 April it sold its services and vehicles to Norgesbuss Invest. It was, however, more successful in New Zealand, where, after gaining a number of tendered services, it opened a new depot at Mount Roskill on 4 May. A few weeks later, on 16 June, Stagecoach sold its Burnley & Pendle Viscount Central coaching unit, together with sixteen vehicles, to local Burnley independent Border Buses. Still seeking expansion, however, on 16 July Stagecoach acquired Thames Transit's 180-bus operations in Oxford and forty-eight-bus Docklands Transit in London, the latter of which was immediately placed under the control of Stagecoach East London. Almost before the ink had dried on the Transit deal, Stagecoach purchased Harry Blundred's Transit Australia's Queensland Sun Bus operations in Cairns, Ipswich and Sunshine Coast together with 120 buses and the depots from which they ran.

Following the sale of its operations in Mombasa, Kenya, due to increasing competition from privately owned minibuses, on 30 August 1997 Stagecoach withdrew completely from Malawi and sold its 51 per cent share to its minority partner Admarc Investments. This was not all, however, as the decision was taken to withdraw from Denmark too, when it sold its Swebus operation, based at Kobenhavn, to its competitor, DSB Busser. Back in the UK, in September Stagecoach Manchester began a new low-cost Magic Bus operation, while on the first day of November it purchased the business and goodwill of Wall's Coaches of Sharston, with whom it, and its predecessor GM Buses South, had competed along Wilmslow Road since deregulation. On this occasion no buses were involved in the deal, leaving Stagecoach Manchester to provide the nineteen vehicles needed to maintain its acquired services. Then, more surprisingly, on 19 December Stagecoach made a successful bid to operate South Yorkshire PTE's loss-making Sheffield Supertram operation on a twenty-seven-year operating concession, believing that it could turn it into a profitable venture in a comparatively short space of time. Under the agreement, the permanent way, depot and rolling stock would remain under the ownership of South Yorkshire Light Rail Ltd, a subsidiary of the PTE. Just before the year ended, on 23 December Stagecoach further strengthened its position in south-east Wales when it purchased Julian Peddle's 58 per cent shareholding in Rhondda Buses, in which it already held a 10 per cent interest. In order to gain full control of the ninety-five-bus company, which traded under the identities of Rhondda Buses, Caerphilly Busways and Parfitts, it also purchased FirstBus' 22 per cent share and Arriva's 10 per cent share. Throughout the year, in addition to adding numerous new buses to its UK fleet, it also cascaded a number of its existing vehicles, including London Leyland Titans, between its subsidiaries to provide a wealth of variety for enthusiasts.

After a quiet start, 1998 burst into life in March when, after having withdrawn from Hong Kong in 1996, Stagecoach made an attempt to return to the colony when it teamed up with China Motor Bus in a joint 50/50 venture. This was unfortunately unsuccessful, as was its bid to acquire MTL Trust Holdings in the UK. On a more positive note, however, Stagecoach purchased a 20 per cent stake in Road King Infrastructure Ltd, a Bermudan-registered company which was listed on the Hong Kong stock exchange and specialised in the development, operation and management of 974 km of toll roads in eight Chinese provinces. Meanwhile, as a result of its growing success, Stagecoach's Swebus operations in Finland were separated in April and as a stand-alone operation renamed Stagecoach Finland. Then, in a surprise move, during that same month, Stagecoach Kenya's twenty tri-axle Dennis Dragon double-deckers were imported into the UK to join Stagecoach Manchester's Magic Bus operation. Still expanding overseas, in August Stagecoach purchased the Yellow Bus Company in Auckland, New Zealand. Then, a month later, Stagecoach acquired Fullers Ferries, who operated nine ferries between Auckland and the surrounding islands. Following this, in October Stagecoach sold its remaining operations in Kenya to a group of local investors and exited the country. Back home, on 10 October Stagecoach purchased a 49 per cent stake in Virgin Rail, who operated the West Coast Main Line and Virgin CrossCountry franchises, thus giving it a further share of the UK's rail market.

1999 saw Stagecoach travel overseas yet again in its bid to expand its global presence. After previously being unsuccessful in its quest to gain a major presence in Hong Kong, it at last achieved its goal in March, when it purchased Hong Kong Citybus and took over its operations on 17 July. In the meantime, on 7 May it acquired a 25 per cent stake in a joint venture with Kwoon Chung Buses, who operated a cross-border service between Hong Kong and China. During the month that followed, Stagecoach returned to North America with its acquisition of the giant Coach USA, who operated subsidised transit services, charter coaches, sightseeing buses and yellow school buses, primarily across the north-east and mid-west. Later, in October, Coach USA acquired the businesses of Erie Coach Lines, Autocar Connaisseur and Trentway-Wagar, rebranding these under the Coach Canada banner, and also operated sightseeing tours in Montreal under the Gray Line identity. However, despite its expansion in Asia and North America, towards the end of 1999 Stagecoach agreed to sell what remained of Swebus to Norwegian-American group Concordia Bus Sweden AB, who took control on the first day of the new millennium.

Since its inception in 1980, as can be seen from the above, Stagecoach has grown rapidly and extensively to become a global bus and coach operator and continued to expand in the UK and beyond during the new millennium, a story which has previously been published by Amberley – *Stagecoach in the Twenty-First Century*.

Without the help of friends for allowing me to use their excellent photographs there would have been numerous gaps in the pictorial content, and thus to all those who have assisted I offer my sincere thanks. The photographs that are uncredited are from my own camera, while those whose name is unfortunately unknown to me are shown as author's collection. To the latter I apologise profusely, and hope that they will forgive me for using their work, but will nevertheless enjoy seeing it in print, as their contribution is massively appreciated.

The first English company to be purchased by Stagecoach was Hampshire Bus, whose Leyland National, 3636 (GFX 975N), is seen here at Barton Park depot, Eastleigh, in April 1987. Seen in its 'as acquired livery', it is accompanied by an unidentified ECW-bodied Bristol LH6L still in NBC colours. (F. W. York)

Standing at Barton Park depot in April 1987 still in the livery of their former owner, South Yorkshire PTE, are Van Hool-McArdle-bodied Volvo Ailsa B55s NAK415/8R and LWB 383P, which had recently been acquired by Hampshire Bus. On the right is Hampshire Bus Bristol FLF6G driver trainer EMR 288D, which had begun life with Wilts & Dorset. (F. W. York)

Also new to South Yorkshire PTE, but having been acquired by Stagecoach from McGill's, Barrhead, is Leyland DAB bendibus 291 (FHE 291V), which is seen here at Winchester while operating for Hampshire Bus.

Starting life with Hants & Dorset in 1978, Hampshire Bus ECW-bodied Bristol VRT 387 (VPR 486S), seen here in Winchester on 24 February 1993, carries a side advert for Stagecoach's short-lived Scotland to London rail operation. (F. W. York)

Wearing a Hampshire Travel fleet name, corporate-liveried Plaxton Paramount 3500-bodied Volvo B10M 1007 (495 FFJ) was originally registered B193 GCA and was transferred to Hampshire Bus from Fife Scottish in 1991. (Campbell Morrison)

A unique bus in the Stagecoach Hampshire Bus fleet was Dodge GO8 43 (D365 OSU), which was fitted with a Wight body with twin welfare-type doors in its rear bulkhead.

Purchased by Hants & Dorset from London Transport via Ensign (dealer) in March 1983, MCW-bodied Leyland Fleetline FE30AGR 1917 (OUC 39R) was transferred by Stagecoach to Cumberland in October 1987, with whom it is seen here still wearing Hampshire Bus livery. (Campbell Morrison)

Displaying CMS Carlislebus lettering on its upper side panels and front roof dome, Cumberland AEC Routemaster 902 (ALD 941B), pictured here together with a Leyland National at Harraby East terminus on 7 April 1988, was acquired by Cumberland from Kelvin Scottish in the summer of 1987. (S. K. Jenkinson)

Purchased by Cumberland from Wallace Arnold, Leeds, in September 1990 when only three years old, Plaxton Paramount 3500-bodied Volvo B10M 157 (WVT 618), which was originally registered D202 LWX, is seen here painted in Shearings Holidays livery for operation under contract to that tours company. (Campbell Morrison)

One of a pair of Alexander-bodied tri-axle Leyland Olympians bought new by Cumberland in 1989, 1201 (F201 FHH) was fitted with ninety-six coach seats. (Campbell Morrison)

One of sixteen Reeve Burgess-bodied Mercedes-Benz L608Ds transferred from Ribble to Cumberland in June 1989, 560 (D560 RCK) is seen here at Bowness while wearing Lakeland Experience livery with 'The Coniston Rambler' lettering above its side windows.

Standing outside Cumberland's Penrith depot on 20 November 1992 are ECW-bodied Bristol VRTs 2024 (DBV 24W), 423 (FAO 423V) and B-series Leyland National 809 (TRN 809V).

Pictured at Bowness Pier on 9 July 1994 while wearing Lakeland Experience livery and lettering, Cumberland's ECW-bodied Bristol VRT 2002 (CBV 2S) was transferred from Ribble in February 1986 and converted to open-top format after being partially de-roofed in an accident in October 1993.

Painted in Cumberland's Coachline livery and seen here in Carlisle in 1994, Duple Laser-bodied Leyland Tiger TRCTL11/3RH 156 (PCK 335) was originally registered B156 WRN and was transferred from Ribble in June 1989.

Wearing United Counties original post-NBC livery, ECW-bodied Bristol VRT 821 (SRP 821N) is pictured here at Northampton bus station in the summer of 1988.

Awaiting their passengers at Biggleswade on 3 May 1989, and showing Stagecoach's corporate livery alongside that of United Counties post-NBC era, are Alexander-bodied Leyland Olympian 633 (F633 MSL) and ECW-bodied Bristol VRT 917 (HBD 917T).

Fully regaled in Stagecoach corporate livery with United Counties lettering on its cove panels is Leyland National 2 582 (NRP 582V) pictured here at Bedford. (Campbell Morrison)

Sporting a United Counties fleet name and Stagecoach Holding Ltd lettering below the logo on its upper-deck side panels is Alexander-bodied 100-seat tri-axle Leyland Olympian 600 (F110 NES), which began life with Magic Bus in Glasgow before transferring to East Midland, and then to United Counties in October 1992. (Campbell Morrison)

Displaying Coachlinks lettering on its side and front panels, United Counties' nine-year-old ECW-bodied Leyland Leopard PSU3G/4R 179 (EBD 179X) is seen here at London Heathrow Airport in July 1991.

When only a week old, Stagecoach United Counties Alexander-bodied Dennis Dart SLF 458 (S458 CVV) with Lo-Liner lettering on its lower side panels is seen here near Northampton bus station on 6 October 1998.

New to Maidstone & District in 1977, Plaxton Derwent-bodied Ford R1014 SKO 273R was purchased by Cumberland with the business of Yeowarts, Whitehaven, in whose livery it is seen here on 24 August 1988. It has been given fleet number 504 by its new owner. (S. A. Jenkinson)

Carrying Cumberland fleet number 561, Plaxton-bodied Leyland Leopard PSU3B/4R LHU 661L, which began life with Bristol Omnibus Co., is seen here wearing the livery of Kirkpatricks, Brigham, from whom it was acquired in May 1988 along with the independent's business.

Seen here on a private hire duty is Cumbria independent Stephenson's of Maryport's Plaxton-bodied Bedford YMT KHH 724W. Stephenson's was acquired by Stagecoach Cumberland on 2 May 1989.

Seen hauling a trailer, corporate-liveried Stagecoach Malawi sixty-one-seat PEW-bodied ERF Trailblazer 863 (BH 5863) was purchased new in 1990. (R. Bailey)

Acquired by Stagecoach Malawi from Kowloon Motor Bus, Hong Kong, in July 1990, thirteen-year-old Met Sec-bodied Daimler CVG6LX-34 1052 (BH 6752) was used in its new home by Cityline. As can be seen, its roof was heavily patched following damage by low vegetation. (R. Bailey)

New to Park Hamilton in March 1988 registered E587 UHS, but acquired by Stagecoach Malawi from Travellers, Hounslow, in January 1991, Plaxton Paramount 3500-bodied Volvo B10M 4 (BH 9604) is seen here fitted with a substantial front bumper and displaying Stagecoach Coachline lettering. (R. Bailey)

Withdrawn Stagecoach Malawi Leyland Victory J216 stands at Blantyre alongside two ex-Kowloon Motor Bus, Hong Kong, Met Sec-bodied Daimler CVG6LX-34s that were acquired solely for cannibalisation in 1989. (R. Bailey)

New in 1979 with Willowbrook 003 bodywork, East Midland Leyland Leopard PSU3E/4R 413 (DWF 23V), seen here at Retford depot on 3 June 1991 while still in its pre-Stagecoach corporate livery, was given its new Duple Dominant body in 1985.

Wearing Mansfield & District fleet names on its pre-Stagecoach livery is East Midland ECW-bodied Bristol VRT 224 (KKY 224W), which was sold to Robinson of Stewkley in September 1999. (Campbell Morrison)

Seen here operating with East Midland subsidiary Frontrunner South East in 1989 is Leyland National 2 36 (VWA 36Y), which returned to its parent owner later that year. (Campbell Morrison)

Having returned to East Midland from its Frontrunner South East operation, ECW-bodied Bristol VRT 158 (SNN 158R) is seen here still displaying its Frontrunner fleet name in 1989. It was transferred to Stagecoach Ribble in October of that year.

Seen at Stockport bus station in 1989 while operating for East Midland subsidiary Frontrunner North West is Alexander-bodied Leyland Atlantean AN68A/1R 431 (KSA 178P), which was new to Grampian in 1976 and was later transferred to Stagecoach Portsmouth.

Leaving East Midland's Clowne depot on 25 October 1990 while undertaking driver training duties is Rainworth Travel Plaxton-bodied Bedford YMT T3 (LPT 872T), which began life with Watson, Annfield Plain, in 1979.

Repainted into East Midland's 1950s livery, former London AEC Routemaster RM1164 (NSG 636A, originally 164 CLT) passes through Clipstone on a journey from Mansfield on 25 October 1990.

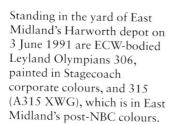

Standing in the yard of East Midland's Harworth depot on 3 June 1991 are ECW-bodied Leyland Olympians 306, painted in Stagecoach corporate colours, and 315 (A315 XWG), which is in East Midland's post-NBC colours.

Resting at Stagecoach East Midland's Chesterfield depot on 3 June 1991 is tri-axle Talbot Pullman E727 UNA, which was new to United Transport Buses at Preston.

Painted in Ribble's post-NBC livery, Leyland National 2 830 (DBV 830W) is pictured here on Talbot Road, Blackpool, on 22 June 1989.

Making its way along Morecambe Promenade on 29 June 1988 is Ribble open-top East Lancs-bodied Leyland Atlantean AN68/1R 1622 (JFR 394N), which started life in 1975 as a conventional closed-top bus with Blackburn Transport.

The first Ribble bus to be repainted into Stagecoach corporate livery was ECW-bodied Leyland Olympian 2157 (A157 OFR), which is seen here at Colne bus station on 15 June 1989.

Transferred from Stagecoach Cumberland to Ribble in December 1991, Alexander-bodied Leyland Tiger TRCTL11/2R 645 (WAO 645Y) lays over at Blackburn bus station on 15 March 1993.

Adorned with Zippy branding, Ribble's former United Transport Buses Robin Hood-bodied
Iveco 49.10 009 (D418 FRV) is seen here leaving Preston bus station on 15 June 1989.

Caught by the camera in Brighton while still wearing Southdown's post-NBC livery is dual-door
Leyland National 44 (RUF 44R). (Author's collection)

Preserved by Stagecoach is Southdown's open-top Brush-bodied Leyland Titan TD1 0813 (UF 4813), which dates from 1929. (Author's collection)

Seen here in August 1989 when only a few weeks old and sporting Southdown's post-NBC livery is Northern Counties-bodied Volvo B10M-50 303 (F303 MYJ).

Repainted into Stagecoach corporate livery with 'Southdown – Part of the Stagecoach Group' fleet names is Leyland National 776 (CBV 776S), which had been transferred from Stagecoach Ribble.

Still adorned in Cedarbus livery, but now owned by Stagecoach Southdown, MCW Metrorider 903 (F563 HPP) is seen here passing through Worthing on its way to Durrington in 1989. (Campbell Morrison)

Seen in 1990 while wearing Stagecoach corporate colours with Portsmouth fleet names is Alexander-bodied Leyland Atlantean AN68A/1R 331 (UOR 331T), which was one of the buses taken over with the Portsmouth Citybus operation.

Former Eastbourne Buses/Topline East Lancs-bodied Leyland Atlantean AN68A/2R 356 (YJK 932V) is pictured here painted in Stagecoach corporate livery with Southdown Portsmouth fleet names.

About to depart from Preston bus station is Mercer of Longridge's MCW-bodied Leyland Fleetline FE30AGR OKW 512R, which was new to South Yorkshire PTE and only remained with Stagecoach Ribble for four months after being taken over in November 1989.

Illustrating Hastings & District's old and new liveries respectively are ECW-bodied Bristol VRTs 523 (PKP 123R) and 524 (PKP 124R), both of which started life with Maidstone & District.

Seen in its home town is Hastings & District's former Maidstone & District ECW-bodied Bristol VRT 559 (BKE 859T).

Preserved by Stagecoach and painted in Hastings & District livery is Park Royal-bodied AEC Regent V 946 (MFN 946F), which started life in the fleet of East Kent Road Car Co. (F. W. York)

New to Ribble before moving to Crosville, Crosville Wales, Northern Bus Company and then to Hastings & District in August 1989, ECW-bodied Bristol RELH6L 414 (PTF 714L) passed to Stagecoach with its purchase of Hastings & District in December 1989.

Seen in July 1992 fitted with Stagecoach Hastings Buses fleet name vinyls but still in its 'as acquired' Hastings & District livery is East Lancs-bodied Bristol VRT 771 (OWE 271K), which began life with Sheffield Corporation.

Still wearing its post-NBC Southdown livery but with a Stagecoach fleet name vinyl on its lower front panel, ECW-bodied Bristol VRT 668 (AAP 668T) is seen in Hastings in June 1993 with foliage caught in its upper-deck window.

One of the new buses purchased by Stagecoach for its Hastings Buses subsidiary in March 1992, corporate-liveried Alexander-bodied Dennis Dart 513 (J513 GCD) is pictured in its home town in July of that year.

Painted in Top Line livery
is Leyland National 403
(PCD 73R), which began life in
the Southdown fleet.

Wearing Southdown's
post-NBC livery and fitted
with Top Line fleet name
vinyls, Leyland National 26
(PCD 126M) stands alongside
Top Line-liveried Leyland
National 12 (MOD 822P),
which had been new to
Western National.

Displaying a Minilink Ribble
fleet name, Carlyle-bodied
Freight Rover Sherpa 128
(D128 NON) was delivered
new to Manchester Minibuses
and is seen here in its home city
in September 1989.

Still painted in East Midland's Frontrunner South East livery, but now operating for Stagecoach Ribble, NCME-bodied Leyland Atlantean AN68A/1R 1684 (LJA 641P) was new to Greater Manchester PTE and is seen here at Blackburn on 25 October 1989.

Collecting its passengers in Preston bus station on 15 June 1989 is former Barrow Borough Transport Leyland National NEO 830R, which is still in its former operator's livery but has had Ribble fleet names added.

Resting at Kempston terminus on 12 August 1988 is ex-London Buses, United Counties AEC Routemaster 705 (68 CLT), which carries a route diagram on its upper-deck side panels and Routemaster lettering on its sides and bonnet front. (S. K. Jenkinson)

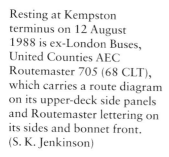

Painted in a branded livery for United Counties Corby's Magic Minis service network is Robin Hood-bodied Iveco 49.10 64 (G64 JVV), which is seen here outside Corby depot on 11 June 1996.

Acquired by Cumberland with the Kirkpatrick's of Brigham business in May 1988, Mellor-bodied Ford Transit D552 URM later served with several Stagecoach companies, including Maun Minibuses, with whom it is seen here. Alongside, a Mercedes-Benz 709D is awaiting a new engine.

Clothed in corporate livery and with Stagecoach Express fleet names is Stagecoach Kenya's locally bodied ERF Trailblazer 901 (KAE 837V). (Author's collection)

This unfortunately poor-quality photograph shows three of Stagecoach Kenya's 1995 Duple Met Sec-bodied Dennis Dragons, all of which were later imported into the UK to join Stagecoach Manchester. (Author's collection)

Having been given an offside entrance door, former Stagecoach Scotland ECW-bodied Bristol FLF6Gs 082 (KPW 482E) and 081 (GDL 769E) await export to Gray Coach Lines, Toronto, Canada, in January 1992. (Campbell Morrison)

Sporting a Coastline fleet name, Robin Hood-bodied Iveco 49.10 920 (G420 RYJ) is seen here at Chichester in 1992.

Seen in April 1993, adorned with Shuttle Bus branding for operation on the service between the Portsmouth ferry terminal, the railway station and the city centre, is Coastline ECW-bodied Bristol VRT 267 (JVW 267W), which began life with Southdown. (F. W. York)

Still wearing the livery in which it was received with the takeover of Alder Valley is Leyland National 253 (NPJ 474R), which was renumbered 1253 by Stagecoach Hants & Surrey. (Author's collection)

Operating on loan to Hampshire Bus, Stagecoach Hants & Surrey ECW-bodied Bristol VRT 616 (GGM 86W) was still clothed in Alder Valley livery when seen here in Basingstoke on 20 February 1993. (F. W. York)

Having been cascaded by Stagecoach Selkent to Stagecoach South Coast Buses in October 1995, freshly repainted Leyland Titan 7237 (EYE 237V) is seen here at Silverhill en route to Hollington. (T. S. Blackman)

New in 1977 to Wellington City Transport (New Zealand), Hawke Hunter-bodied Leyland Leopard PSU3C/2R 412 (IL 4519), seen here in Stagecoach corporate livery, unbelievably remained in service until 2005. (Author's collection)

One of sixty-eight Hawke-bodied Volvo B58/ Brown Boveri trolleybuses taken over by Stagecoach from Wellington City Transport (New Zealand) in 1992, 210 (KA 9109), which was new in 1983, is seen here in its new owner's corporate livery. (Author's collection)

Painted in Stagecoach corporate livery, Coachwork International-bodied Renault S75 minibus 291 (PD 1038) is seen here when new in 1990, lettered for Cityline Hutt Valley (New Zealand). (Stagecoach International)

1983 vintage MAN SG220 bendibus 2004 (KR 6018) looks immaculate in its corporate Stagecoach Auckland (New Zealand) colours. (Author's collection)

Stagecoach East Midland ECW-bodied Leyland Olympian 326 (C326 HWJ) is seen in Mansfield bus station while displaying Midland Travel fleet names on 3 June 1991.

With a poster on its upper-deck side panels promoting Stagecoach's forthcoming launch on the London Stock Market is Ribble ECW-bodied Leyland Atlantean AN68/1R 1477 (TRN 477V). It is seen here resting in Preston bus station on 2 April 1993.

Standing in the yard of Stagecoach's Blackburn depot on 7 September 1993 is ex-Lancaster City Transport East Lancs-bodied Leyland Atlantean AN68D/2R A214 MCK. It still in its former owner's livery but with Ribble Buses fleet names and the fleet number 1214.

Posed in the doorway of Stagecoach's ex-Lancaster City Transport depot at Morecambe on 28 March 1999 is Alexander PS-bodied Volvo B10M 699 (K699 ERM), which was new to Cumberland but is seen here with Stagecoach Lancaster fleet names.

Awaiting its passengers in Hastings in September 1993, a few days after being taken over by Stagecoach, is East Kent Willowbrook-bodied Bristol VRT 7991 (TFN 991T).

Resting between duties at Canterbury bus station on 17 August 1994 is Stagecoach East Kent Leyland National 1183 (NFN 83R). It is seen still in the livery of its former owner. (F. W. York)

Parked in Canterbury bus station on 17 August 1994 are Stagecoach East Kent ECW-bodied Bristol VRT 7651 (XJJ 651V), which has been repainted into its new owner's corporate livery, and Northern Counties-bodied Leyland Olympian 7810 (H810 BKK), which still wears its original owner's colours. (F. W. York)

Painted in National Express corporate livery, and seen here passing through Lewisham on its way to Ramsgate on 4 May 1997, is Stagecoach East Kent Van Hool-bodied Volvo B10M 8503 (IIL 3503). (D. W. Rhodes)

Seen displaying an East Kent Coaches title on its side panels when new in 1995 is Stagecoach East Kent Plaxton Premier-bodied Volvo B10M 8408 (M408 BFG). (T. W. W. Knowles)

Still painted in Stagecoach London livery, Leyland Titan NUW 596Y is seen here at Havant, en route to The Hard, Portsmouth, on 7 November 1995. It has been cascaded to Stagecoach Coastline and renumbered 7296. (F. W. York)

Stagecoach Grimsby Cleethorpes MCW Metrorider 45 (E45 HFE) is pictured here still wearing its original owner's livery together with GCT logos.

Fitted with Roe dual-door bodywork, Leyland Fleetline FE30AGR 129 (XFU 129V), seen here on 7 July 1994, continues to wear Grimsby Cleethorpes Transport livery, complete with logos, eight months after the undertaking was purchased by Stagecoach.

Standing in Cleethorpes on 7 July 1994, and both repainted into Stagecoach corporate livery, are former Grimsby Cleethorpes Transport East Lancs-bodied Dennis Lance 5 (L705 HFU) and Alexander-bodied Dennis Dominator 75 (F75 TFU).

Soon after Stagecoach purchased Grimsby Cleethorpes Transport, Roe-bodied Leyland Fleetline FE30AGR 113 (MBE 113R) was converted to open-top configuration and it is seen here at Pleasure Island, Cleethorpes, in August 1994.

With a National 3 badge fitted below its windscreen, City of Gloucester Leyland National 3060 (TAE 624S) is seen in Cheltenham in April 1994, painted in its pre-Stagecoach livery, followed by Roe-bodied Leyland Olympian 9519 (LW S35Y), which is in corporate colours.

Wearing Cheltenham & Gloucester's Metro minibus livery, Alexander-bodied Mercedes-Benz L608D 656 (C656 XDF) is followed through Cheltenham in April 1994 by Alexander-bodied Ford Transit 627 (C627 SFH).

Despite now being under Stagecoach ownership, seen resting in Gloucester bus station are City of Gloucester Leyland National 3039 (NOE 585R), which started life with Midland Red, and ECW-bodied Bristol VRT 5621 (VOD 593S), which was new to Western National.

Showing off its Cheltenham District livery, Stagecoach Leyland National 3500 (AAE 644V) is seen here in Gloucester bus station in the spring of 1994.

Freshly repainted in Stagecoach corporate livery, Stagecoach Gloucester Roe-bodied Leyland Olympian 9519 (LWS 35Y), which was originally part of the Bristol Omnibus Co. fleet, awaits its passengers in Cheltenham in April 1994.

Seen collecting a respectable number of passengers, and displaying route branding on its side panels, is Stagecoach Cheltenham District Alexander-bodied Volvo B6 847 (M847 HDF).

Caught on camera in Cirencester, still in its pre-Stagecoach livery, is Stroud District Leyland National SD3046 (PHW 988S).

Painted in its post-NBC livery and resting at Stagecoach's Stroud depot is ECW-bodied Bristol VRT SD5535 (EWS 743W).

Originally operated by West Yorkshire PTE, Roe-bodied Leyland Olympian 9507 (UWW 7X) is seen here painted in its post-NBC, pre-Stagecoach, Swindon District livery.

After being transferred from Stagecoach Western Buses to Stagecoach Midland Red, Leyland National 806 (WAS 771V), which started life with Ayrshire independent AA Buses, is seen on 6 October 1998. It is still in its original owner's livery, but it has had Stagecoach Midland Red fleet names added.

Seen at Stagecoach's Cheltenham depot on 13 April 1997 while wearing an unrelieved blue livery for use on Cheltenham District contract duties is ECW-bodied Bristol VRT 215 (XDV 602S), which was new to Western National in 1978.

Seen being operated by Circle Line in Cheltenham in April 1994 is Optare-bodied Leyland Cub CU435 C810 KBT, which began life in 1986 with West Yorkshire PTE.

New to Bristol Omnibus Co. in October 1976, dual-door ECW-bodied Bristol VRT 5068 (MOU 742R) is seen in Gloucester bus station while being operated by Circle Line.

Seen at Chipping Norton while operating a school service in May 1994, and still painted in pre-Stagecoach colours, is Midland Red South ECW-bodied Bristol VRT 943 (GTX 754W), which had started life with National Welsh. (T. W. W. Knowles)

Wearing Stratford Blue livery, fleet names and a Park & Ride poster on its side panels, Stagecoach Midland Red Wright-bodied Mercedes-Benz 811D 408 (J408 PRW) is seen in Stratford-upon-Avon, en route to Leamington via Warwick. (F. W. York)

Resting in Coventry on 6 October 1998 are Stagecoach Midland Red ECW-bodied Bristol VRT 928 (LHT 725P), which began life with Bristol Omnibus Co., and former Vanguard of Bedworth East Lancs-bodied Leyland PSU3E/2R 18 (YBO 18T), which was new to Rhymney Valley in 1979. Neither survived long enough to receive Stagecoach corporate livery.

Still painted in the livery of G&G Travel, Leamington Spa, former West Midlands PTE MCW-bodied Leyland Fleetline FE30AGR WDA 994T was another bus that never gained Stagecoach corporate livery.

New to Crosville and later acquired by Bedworth independent, Vanguard, Leyland National LMA 411T is seen here in Coventry after gaining Stagecoach corporate livery, albeit with the Vanguard name in its nearside windscreen. (Campbell Morrison)

New to Ralph of Langley, with whom it was registered F481 FUA, Stagecoach Midland Red coach-seated Optare-bodied Mercedes-Benz 811D 426 (CSV 219) is pictured here at Leamington Spa on 6 October 1998.

Lined up in the yard of Stagecoach Midland Red's Leamington depot on 6 October 1998 are ex-Busways Alexander-bodied Leyland Atlantean AN68A/2R 982 (AVK 174V), former United Counties Leyland National 809 (SVV 589W) and Alexander (Belfast)-bodied Mercedes-Benz 709D 335 (M335 LHP).

Adorned with Primeline branding and displaying route information on its cover panels, Stagecoach Midland Red Alexander-bodied Dennis Dart SLF 154 (R154 CRW) is seen in Coventry on 6 October 1998.

Leaving Pool Meadow bus station, Coventry, on 6 October 1998 is Stagecoach Midland Red Alexander PS-bodied Volvo B10M 220 (P220 HBD) with Travelwise branding on its side panels.

Seen passing through Cwmbran en route to Newport, and still painted in its Red & White livery but with a Stagecoach label on the lower edge of its foremost nearside window, is Carlyle-bodied Freight Rover Sherpa 120 (E120 RAX).

Wearing Red & White livery as it awaits its passengers in Merthyr Tydfil bus station in April 1994 is a Stagecoach Red & White Dormobile-bodied Ford Transit 269 (C471 BHY), which began life with Bristol Omnibus Co.

Heading to Monmouth, still in the livery of its previous owner, is Stagecoach Red & White Leyland National N644 (BUV 209V), which was delivered new to National Welsh.

With route details on its side windows and displaying a Stagecoach 2000 name is Stagecoach Red & White corporate-liveried Plaxton-bodied Volvo B10M 773 (P773 TTG). It is seen here at Merthyr Tydfil bus station on 12 April 1997.

Standing in the yard of Stagecoach Red & White's Cwmbran depot on 12 April 1997, still showing the GMS logo of its former owner in its front nearside upper-deck window, is NCME-bodied Leyland Atlantean AN68A/1R 871 (VBA 166S).

New to the armed forces, and later used by Grey Green, Stagecoach Transit Wadham Stringer-bodied Dodge G13 17 (D157 HHN), seen here at Stockton depot on 24 November 1999, was one of several buses of this type purchased by Stagecoach for use as driver trainers.

Resting at Stagecoach Red & White's Bulwark depot, Chepstow, on 12 April 1997 are ex-Stagecoach Busways Alexander-bodied Leyland Atlantean AN68A/2R 870 (AVK 173V) and Alexander-bodied Bristol VRT 861 (OSR 206R), which began life with Tayside Regional Council before passing to National Welsh and thence to Red & White.

Seen awaiting delivery to Stagecoach Hong Kong in December 1993 are five unregistered Alexander PS-bodied Volvo B10Ms, all of which carry air conditioning pods on their roof. (Campbell Morrison)

The second of six 110-seat Alexander-bodied tri-axle Volvo Olympians new to Stagecoach Hong Kong in May 1995, 7 (GK 2009) is seen here in service in its new home in August of that year. All were sold to Hong Kong Citybus on 31 March 1997 when Stagecoach withdrew from the colony.

Competitors standing at the Hazel Grove terminus of route 192 on 5 May 1994 are Stagecoach Manchester Alexander-bodied Volvo B6 255 (L255 CCK) and GM Buses South's Northern Counties-bodied Leyland Olympian 3058 (B58 PJA). Ironically, GM Buses South was to become part of the Stagecoach Group nine months later.

Still wearing Newcastle Busways livery, but sporting a 'Part of the Stagecoach Group' strapline below its fleet name, is Alexander-bodied Leyland Olympian 630 (C630 LFT). It has been fitted with a 'help' bumper at the base of its lower front panel.

Ten-year-old Reeve Burgess-bodied Mercedes-Benz 709D 1429 (E429 AFT), with 'Newcastle Busways – Part of the Stagecoach Group' fleet name, is seen here leaving Wallsend bus station on 30 April 1997.

Newcastle Busways-liveried Plaxton-bodied Dennis Lance 1201 (M201 DRG) stands at South Shields Market Place in front of a South Shields Busways Dennis Dart on 25 October 1995.

Showing the Sunderland variant of the Busways livery on 8 April 1995 is Stagecoach's Plaxton-bodied Dennis Lance 1203 (M203 DRG).

Pictured leaving the DHSS complex at Benton on 1 September 1993, still in Newcastle Busways livery but with a Favourite fleet name after being cascaded to the low-cost unit, is Alexander-bodied Leyland Atlantean AN68A/2R 262 (SCN 262S), which was new in 1978.

Starting life with Lancashire United, and seen here on 3 November 1995 with Stagecoach Busways' low-cost Favourite unit, is Plaxton-bodied Leyland Leopard PSU3E/4R 1896 (OTD 825R).

Employed by another of Stagecoach Busways' operating units, Economic, Northern Counties-bodied Leyland Olympian 676 (H676 HNL) is seen here leaving the old Sunderland bus station. (Campbell Morrison)

Resting at Eldon Square, Newcastle, on 23 March 1994 are two members of Stagecoach Busways Blue Bus Services low-cost unit. ECW-bodied Bristol RESL6G 1818 (JMW 167P) originated with Thamesdown Transport, while ECW-bodied Bristol LHS6L 1607 (TPJ 64S), standing alongside, had begun life with London Country.

Seen here as part of Stagecoach Busways' Armstrong Galley coaching subsidiary is Plaxton Paramount 3500-bodied Leyland Tiger 14 (644 HKX).

Painted in Stagecoach Busways Economic livery but sporting Blue Bus Services fleet names is Plaxton-bodied Dennis Dart 1753 (L753 VNL), seen here passing along Gallowgate, Newcastle-upon-Tyne.

Wearing a dedicated livery for the MetroCentre Shuttle service is Stagecoach Newcastle Busways Optare-bodied Dennis Lance 1204 (M204 DRG).

Seen in Blackett Street, Newcastle, on 7 December 1996, carrying all-over advertising for the National Express Newcastle to London service, is Stagecoach Busways Alexander-bodied Leyland Olympian 641 (C641 LFT).

Enjoying a break at Eldon Square, Newcastle, on 7 December 1996 is Stagecoach Busways corporate-liveried Northern Counties-bodied Scania L113CRL 952 (M952 DRG).

Approaching Meadowhall bus station in October 1994 is part Stagecoach-owned South Yorkshire PTE's Alexander-bodied Dennis Dominator 2487 (D487 OWE).

New to Cumberland, Leyland National 2 WAO 397Y is seen after being transferred to Circle Line at Gloucester and repainted into its green and white livery.

Stagecoach East London Leyland National LS403 (BYW 403V) rests outside Lambourne House, Romford, after being converted to a mobility bus. (Campbell Morrison)

Passing Marble Arch, London, Stagecoach East London AEC Routemaster RML2705 (SMK 705F) proudly shows off its new gold fleet name.

Stagecoach East London front-entrance AEC Routemaster RMA8 (NMY 640E), which was new to BEA, is seen operating route 15 before it became an RM-operated heritage service. (Author's collection)

Posed for the camera in Stagecoach East London's North Street garage, Romford, on 13 April 1996, are Green Line Routemaster RMC461 (461 CLT), Leyland Titans T1 (THX 401S) and T511 (KYV 511X), AEC Routemaster RML2760 (SMK 760F) and Leyland Titan T288 (KYN 288X), the latter of which wears Stagecoach's corporate livery.

Stagecoach East London Leyland Titan T261 (GYE 261W) is seen here circumnavigating Marble Arch on its way to Hackney Wick.

Displaying an East London Hoppa name on its side panels, Stagecoach East London Alexander Dash-bodied Dennis Dart DAL23 (N323 AMC) is seen heading for the Barking garage terminus of route 238. (Author's collection)

Making its way through Piccadilly London, in May 1995 is Stagecoach East London Northern Counties-bodied Scania N113DRB S37 (J137 HMT). (D. W. Rhodes)

Freshly repainted and waiting to receive its destination blinds, Stagecoach Selkent Leyland Titan T770 (OHV 770Y) stands in the yard of Catford garage in September 1996. (J. A. Godwin/G. Matthews)

Stagecoach Selkent LV1 (L201 YAG) was a Plaxton-bodied Dennis Lance that was later converted to single-door layout by Alexander (coachbuilder) before being transferred to Stagecoach Ribble. (Author's collection)

Collecting its Lewisham-bound passengers is Stagecoach Selkent Leyland Olympian L263 (D367 JJD), which numerically carried the last body to be built by ECW before it closed in January 1987. (J. A. Godwin/G. Matthews)

New to London Buses in March 1993, Van Hool-bodied DAF MB230 DV38 (K538 RJX), with Selkent Travel fleet names, passed to Stagecoach Selkent in September 1994. (Campbell Morrison)

Seen in Stockton-on-Tees High Street on 8 April 1995 with 'Transit – Part of the Stagecoach Group' lettering on its side panels is Northern Counties-bodied Renault S56 337 (F337 VEF).

Sporting Cleveland Coaches livery and fleet names, Stagecoach Transit ECW-bodied Leyland Olympian 983 (PJI 4983) is seen here in Newcastle-upon-Tyne on a dismal day in November 1994. New to Alder Valley, with whom it was registered B577 LPE, it was acquired by Cleveland Transit from Clyde Coast Coaches, Ardrossan.

Resting in Stagecoach Transit's Stockton-on-Tees depot on 8 April 1995 is NCME-bodied Leyland Titan PD3/4 500 (PRX 189B), which began life in May 1964 with Southdown, with whom it was registered 417 DCD.

Heading through Stockton-on-Tees on 30 April 1997 and wearing its new owner's corporate livery is Stagecoach Transit Leyland Lynx 2 627 (K627 YVN).

Cascaded from Stagecoach East London and seen here in the High Street in Stockton-on-Tees on 24 November 1999 is Leyland Titan 283 (A826 SUL), which was loaned to Stagecoach Red & White before reaching its new Teesside home in the summer of 1998.

Although new to Stagecoach Kingston upon Hull in April 1995, Northern Counties-bodied Volvo B10M 710 (M710 KRH) sports a KHCT fleet name, albeit with a 'Part of the Stagecoach Group' strapline. (Campbell Morrison)

Also displaying a KHCT fleet name in the spring of 1995 is Stagecoach Kingston upon Hull MCW Metrobus 515 (LAT 515V), which was new in May 1980. (Campbell Morrison)

Having gained a Stagecoach Kingston upon Hull fleet name, but still wearing its former municipal-owner's fleet name, MCW Metrobus 520 (SAG520W) stands outside former KHCT's offices on 10 October 1996.

Used on mobility bus services and carrying a Handyrider fleet name and seen at Hull's Paragon bus park on 11 October 1996, Stagecoach Kingston upon Hull Duple-bodied Dennis Lancet 61 (YAY 21Y) was new to Leicester City Transport in December 1982.

Standing in the yard of Stagecoach Kingston upon Hull's depot on 27 March 1999, and illustrating new and old liveries, are Stagecoach Express-liveried Plaxton-bodied Volvo B10M 81 (P181 PRH), Alexander-bodied Dennis Dominator 209 (B109 UAT), East Lancs-bodied Dennis Dominator 231 (C131 CAT) and East Lancs-bodied Scania N112CR 704 (F704 BAT).

Painted in corporate livery, Stagecoach Kingston upon Hull East Lancs-bodied Scania N112CR 710 (F701 BAT) rests alongside Hull railway station on 11 October 1996.

Heading through Darlington on 16 November 1994, followed by Stagecoach corporate-liveried Leyland National 2129 (UHG 739R), is Carlyle-bodied Iveco 49.19 1659 (F659 KNL), which is still wearing the colours of the Stagecoach Busways Blue Bus Services subsidiary, from whom it had been transferred for the Darlington free bus operation.

Painted in corporate colours with a Stagecoach Darlington fleet name, ex-Stagecoach Busways Alexander-bodied Leyland Fleetline FE30AGR 815 (OCU 815R) operates one of the free bus services in Darlington on 16 November 1994.

New to Ribble, Stagecoach Darlington's Reeve Burgess-bodied Mercedes-Benz L608D 356 (D526 RCK) rests at its depot on 20 October 1995 together with Duple Goldliner-bodied Leyland Tiger TRCTL11/3R 189 (PES 189Y, originally SFS 582Y), which had been transferred from Stagecoach Fife.

New to Barrow Borough Transport, and later operating with Stagecoach Ribble, Leyland National 2122 (NEO 833R) is seen here operating the free bus service with Stagecoach Darlington on 16 November 1994.

Still painted in the livery of its former owner, Hartlepool Transport, Stagecoach Hartlepool ECW-bodied Bristol RELL6L 80 (SEF 80L) was already twenty-two years old when seen in its home town on 8 April 1995.

Also new to Hartlepool Transport, but now wearing its new owner's corporate livery, is Stagecoach Hartlepool Northern Counties-bodied Dennis Falcon H 28 (B28 PA). It is seen here in Church Street, Hartlepool, on 8 April 1995.

Stagecoach Hartlepool dual-door Leyland National 2 18 (KAJ 18W), caught on camera on 8 April 1995, began life with Hartlepool Transport in October 1980.

Stagecoach Hartlepool ultimately reintroduced double-deckers to the town, as illustrated by NCME-bodied Leyland FE30AGR 131 (GAJ 131V), which had been transferred from Stagecoach Transit. It is seen here at Hart Station on 30 April 1997.

Acquired by Stagecoach East Midland with the municipal business of Chesterfield Transport, in whose livery it is seen here in January 1996, is Leyland National 36 (WBN 484T), which began life with Lancashire United. (P. T. Stokes)

Displaying Spire Sprinter lettering on its Chesterfield Transport livery is Alexander-bodied Mercedes-Benz 811D 17 (J217 AET), which was taken into Stagecoach East Midland's fleet. (Author's collection)

Depositing its passengers in Retford bus station, and still wearing Chesterfield Transport livery together with a Retford & District fleet name, is Stagecoach East Midland Alexander-bodied Leyland Leopard PSU3C/3R 202 (OSJ 632R), which started life north of the border with Western SMT. (P. T. Stokes)

East Midland subsidiary Whites of Calver's Plaxton-bodied Bedford YMT FTO 550V, which originated from the fleet of Barton Transport, Chilwell, is seen on a private hire duty in Bradford.

Awaiting its departure from Haymarket bus station, Newcastle-upon-Tyne, to Middlesbrough in 1994 is Transit subsidiary Cleveland Coaches Plaxton-bodied Leyland Leopard PSU3E/4R 902 (BPY 402T). Its destination box is mounted on its front roof dome.

Representing Stagecoach Grimsby & Cleethorpes' coaching subsidiary, Peter Sheffield, is Duple Laser-bodied Leyland Tiger PSU 764.

Resting at Cambus' Cambridge depot, having been painted in their owner's post-NBC livery in pre-Stagecoach days, are Leyland Nationals PTD 671S and NEN 954R – both of which were new to Lancashire United. NCME-bodied Daimler Fleetline CRG6LXB 802 (PRJ 499R), which began life with Greater Manchester PTE, is also present.

Heading to Cambridge railway station painted in a dedicated City Rail Link livery, Stagecoach Cambus Marshall-bodied Volvo B6 669 (L669 MFL) is seen overtaking Optare MetroRider 978 (M978 WWR) in Cambridge on 11 June 1996.

Leaving Drummer Street bus station, Cambridge, on 11 June 1996 in pre-corporate livery, is Stagecoach Cambus ECW-bodied Bristol VRT 733 (JUB 650V), which started life with West Yorkshire Road Car Co.

Wearing Millerbus livery but displaying Stagecoach Cambus fleet names, Leyland National 2 304 (PEX 620W) leaves Cambridge's Drummer Street bus station on 11 June 1996.

Seen on 11 June 1996 with lettering for Cambridge's Park & Ride operation on its side panels and sporting a Millerbus fleet name, Stagecoach Cambus Leyland Lynx 311 (F168 SMT) was new to the erstwhile independent in January 1989.

Operating Cambridge's free city centre shuttle service, CNG-powered Optare MetroRider 81, appropriately registered GAZ 4381, collects its passengers in Emmanuel Street on 11 June 1996, its first day in service.

Intended for Stagecoach Western Buses when new in February 1996, Alexander (Belfast)-bodied Mercedes-Benz 709D 209 (N642 VSS) was instead diverted to Stagecoach Cambus, with whom it is seen here on 11 June 1996.

New to Eastern Counties Omnibus Co., coach-seated ECW-Bristol VRT 754 (VEX 291X) looks superb in its Stagecoach Viscount Buses livery as it rests in Peterborough on 12 June 1996.

Wearing Peterborough Bus Company livery and fleet name, Stagecoach Viscount ECW-bodied Leyland Olympian 482 (A561 KWY), seen here on 14 April 1996, began life with West Riding Automobile Company.

New to Eastern Counties Omnibus Co., but seen here with a Peterborough & District fleet name after being preserved by Cambus, ECW-bodied Bristol FLF6G FLF453 (JAH 553D) has now become part of Stagecoach's heritage fleet and has gained the group's current corporate livery.

Resting in Stagecoach Viscount's Peterborough depot on 14 April 1996 in three different liveries are ECW-bodied Leyland Olympian 482 (A561 KWY), former Western National ECW-bodied Bristol VRT 713 (LOD 723P) – which is sporting a Stagecoach Viscount fleet name – and an unidentified Viscount-liveried Bristol VRT.

Seen en route to Wolverton, Buckinghamshire, Road Car ECW-bodied Bristol VRT 3436 (OUD 436M) started life with City of Oxford, but later served with Western National before joining Milton Keynes Citybus in 1992. (Campbell Morrison)

Leaving the old, and now closed, Milton Keynes bus station on 1 October 1996 is Stagecoach subsidiary Buckinghamshire Road Car Leyland National 2 2622 (PEX 622W), which was new to Eastern Counties.

Stagecoach subsidiary's Milton Keynes City Bus Robin Hood-bodied Mercedes-Benz L608D 19 (D119 VRP) heads through the rural outskirts of Milton Keynes en route to the central bus station. (Author's collection)

Stagecoach Portugal UTIC-AEC 183 (EL-44-91) is seen here in Estoril before receiving corporate livery. (Author's collection)

Hiding Stagecoach Portugal's two open-top, front-entrance Routemasters, which were new to BEA, is UTIC-AEC 830, which has route branding on its side panels. (Author's collection)

Built at York by British Rail in the early 1970s, and later given a facelift, Stagecoach South West Trains corporate-liveried Class 423/1 EMU No. 3567 is seen at Portsmouth on 29 April 1999. (F. W. York)

Still wearing Bayline livery, Robin Hood-bodied Ford Transit 492 (C492 FFJ) heads through Torquay on a local service.

Built for Devon General as a convertible open-top ECW-bodied Bristol VRT, 935 (VDV 135S), with a Bayline fleet name, is seen with its roof removed in Torquay on a sunny summer's day.

Resting in Exeter bus station are two Reeve Burgess-bodied Mercedes-Benz 709Ds: 73 (F733 FDV), with Devon General fleet names; and 56 (F718 FDV), with Bayline identity. (F. W. York)

Wearing Devon General fleet names and its pre-Stagecoach livery is ECW-bodied Bristol VRT 1196 (FDV 840V), which was later transferred to Stagecoach Scotland at Perth. (Campbell Morrison)

Seen on 4 April 1995 at Stagecoach Transit's Stockton-on-Tees depot in use as a driver trainer, Alexander-bodied Leyland Leopard PSU3C/3R 501 (XMS 253R) was new to Alexander (Midland) in March 1977 and was acquired by Cleveland Transit from Skillplace Mid West at Swindon in 1994. It later passed to Stagecoach Cambus for continued driver training and was repainted into Stagecoach's corporate livery.

Built by British Rail Engineering in July 1973 and leased by Porterbrook to Virgin Trains in 1997, Class 87 No. 87004, seen here under the wires on the West Coast Main Line, was sold for further use in Bulgaria in 2008. (Author's collection)

Standing in Piccadilly bus station, Manchester, in April 1996, and still in its GM Buses South livery, is Stagecoach Manchester Northern Counties-bodied Leyland Olympian 3087 (B87 SJA).

Representing Stagecoach Manchester's Charterplan coaching unit is Plaxton Paramount 3500-bodied Leyland Tiger TRCTL11/3RH TPX 884, which was originally registered B371 VBA. (Author's collection)

Having gained its new owner's corporate livery, Stagecoach Manchester's former GM Buses South MCW Metrobus 5173 (ANA 173Y) is pictured on the 204 service to Hyde in November 1998.

Seen in Manchester Piccadilly bus station in the summer of 1996 when only a few weeks old is 806 (N806 DNE), one of a large fleet of Alexander PS-bodied Volvo B10Ms operated by Stagecoach Manchester. (T. W. W. Knowles)

Another Stagecoach Manchester bus seen in Piccadilly bus station when comparatively new is Alexander-bodied Volvo Olympian 721 (P721 GND), which was purchased new in October 1996. (J. A. Godwin)

Having begun life with National Welsh, Leyland National 2 (BUH 239V) was acquired by Burnley & Pendle, with whom it is seen in Burnley bus station in October 1996, numbered 69.

Seen collecting its passengers in Burnley bus station in October 1996 while painted in Wizard livery is part Stagecoach-owned Burnley & Pendle Robin Hood-bodied Mercedes-Benz 811D 88 (E88 HRN).

New to Tayside, Alexander-bodied Bristol VRT OSR 197R was acquired by Burnley & Pendle at a comparatively young age and, numbered 197, it is seen here in Burnley bus station in October 1996.

Seen painted in Burnley & Pendle's coaching subsidiary Viscount Central's livery in October 1996 is Alexander-bodied Volvo B10M-50 115 (H115 ABV), which was purchased new in February 1991.

Entering Accrington bus station in October 1996 after joining Stagecoach is East Lancs-bodied Leyland Atlantean AN68/1R 194 (KHG 194T), still in its previous owner Hyndburn Transport's livery.

Resting at Hyndburn Transport's depot in November 1996 are four of the company's vehicles, all of which had been acquired second-hand. Alexander-bodied Leyland Atlantean AN68/2R 210 (GBV 110N) had started life with Preston Corporation, while Willowbrook-bodied Leyland Atlantean AN68B/1R 140 (WWM 920W) was new to Merseyside PTE. Meanwhile, Duple-bodied Leyland Leopard coaches – PSU3E/4R 57 (WWM 576W) and PSU3F/4R 55 (VNH 157W), both of which have had 'A Stagecoach Subsidiary' strapline added to their fleet name – were acquired from Merseyside PTE and United Counties respectively.

Seen in its pre-Stagecoach livery is Swebus triple-door Volvo 133 (NBU 875). (Author's collection)

Carrying Swebus Finland fleet names on its Stagecoach corporate livery is tri-axle Volvo 137 (JCX 962). (Author's collection)

Awaiting its passengers at Sandown station on Stagecoach's Isle of Wight's Island Line is No. 004, a former London Transport Northern Line Underground train, which was built by Metro-Cammell in October 1939. (Author's collection)

Promoting low-cost travel on Tyneside, Stagecoach Busways Alexander-bodied Leyland Atlantean AN68C/2R 214 (EJR 114W), seen here on 30 April 1997, was one of a number of elderly double-deckers repainted into Magic Bus livery to compete with independent HMB Buses.

Wearing Thames Transit livery, and looking somewhat scruffy, is Mellor-bodied Ford Transit 104 (D104 PTT). (T. W. W. Knowles)

New to Bayline, Thames Transit Mellor-bodied Iveco 59.12 2066 (L318 BOD) rests between duties in the pouring rain in Oxford. (Campbell Morrison)

Heading a line of Stagecoach Oxford Tube coaches at Grosvenor Gardens, London, is Ikarus Blue Danube-bodied Volvo B10M 24 (F24 LBW), which was new to McLean, Witney. Having suffered damage to its lower front panel, it is a far cry from the coaches used on this prestigious service today.

Branded for 'The Rose Hill Runner' service in Oxford, and still sporting Thames Transit fleet names, is Stagecoach Oxford Plaxton-bodied Dennis Dart 3026 (M75 VJO). (D. W. Rhodes)

Having been repainted into corporate colours, Stagecoach Oxford Carlyle-bodied Mercedes-Benz 811D 362 (G838 UDV) had begun life with Burtons of Brixham, and later served with Bayline at Torquay.

New to Red Admiral, Docklands Minibus's 394 (H785 GTA), seen here en route to Barking on route 368, is a Carlyle-bodied Mercedes-Benz 811D. (Sam Tillson collection)

Purchased new by Citybus, Hong Kong, in August 1995, Plaxton Pointer-bodied Dennis Dart GM 6788 was repatriated to the UK to join Stagecoach Coastline in December 1999. Registered N998 RCD and then re-registered 406 DCD, it is seen here en route to Portsmouth with route 21 and Sainsbury's branding, and clearly shows its roof-mounted air conditioning pod. (F. W. York)

Looking immaculate is Cairns, Queensland, Australia Sunbus Mercedes-Benz 0815 5557 (982 LAX), which is fitted with Bustech bodywork. (Author's collection)

Painted in Magic Bus livery with added route 192 branding, Stagecoach Manchester Northern Counties-bodied Leyland Olympian 3010 (ANA 10Y) is seen in December 1999.

Stagecoach Supertram No. 08, still in its 'as acquired' livery, departs from Meadowhall, Sheffield, en route to Herdings Park on 14 May 1998.

Also leaving Meadowhall on 14 May 1998, and passing beneath the M1 motorway Tinsley flyover on its way to Middlewood, is Stagecoach Supertram No. 107, which had recently been repainted into its owner's corporate livery.

Resting between duties in Cardiff bus station is Rhondda Volvo B10M 704 (A14 RBL), which had started life with Fife Scottish as a double-deck coach registered B176 FFS. It had been given its new East Lancs body in November 1995 before joining Stagecoach in Wales.

Rhondda Buses subsidiary Caerphilly Busways Plaxton Pointer-bodied Volvo B6 714 (M74 HHB) is pictured here in June 1998.

In 1996 Stagecoach introduced coach-seated bendibuses to its UK fleet. Seen branded for the 909 service from Hull to Doncaster in June 1999 is Cleveland Transit Jonckheere Modulo-bodied Volvo B10MA-55 97 (T97 JHN), which was being operated by Stagecoach Kingston upon Hull. (R. G. Pope)

Wearing Stagecoach Cumberland's Coachline livery, Plaxton 3500-bodied Volvo B10M 109 (WLT 706), which was originally registered C109 OHH, rests in the yard of Stagecoach's Morecambe depot on 28 March 1999.

Representing Auckland (New Zealand)-based 'The Yellow Bus Company' is dual-door Mercedes-Benz 0302 1026 (JA2138). (Author's collection)

Bought new by Kingston upon Hull City Transport as a mobility bus, Leyland National 2 60 (B60 WKH) is seen on 27 March 1999 after receiving Stagecoach corporate livery and Handyrider branding.

Seen painted in pre-Stagecoach KHCT livery but displaying Stagecoach Kingston upon Hull fleet names on 27 March 1999, East Lancs-bodied Scania N112DRB 800 (C100 HSJ) was inherited by Stagecoach Western Scottish in 1995 with the fleet of A1 Service, Ardrossan, in which it was owned by Brown, Dreghorn.

Having started life with Stagecoach Kenya, Duple MetSec-bodied tri-axle Dennis Dragon 684 (M684 TDB) was imported by Stagecoach Manchester, in whose Magic Bus livery it is seen in Piccadilly bus station, Manchester, in November 1998.

Painted in a black- and gold-branded livery for the Uni-Sprint service to Lancaster University is Stagecoach Lancaster Alexander-bodied Leyland Olympian 2192 (H192 WFR). It is seen here inside its owner's Morecambe depot on 28 March 1999.

Branded for the Skyline service from Manchester city centre to the airport, Stagecoach Manchester Alexander-bodied MAN 18.220 158 (S158 TRJ) awaits its departure from Piccadilly bus station, Manchester, on a wet December day in 1999.

Seen at Luton Airport on 27 May 1999, branded for the Virgin Trains rail link service from Milton Keynes, is Stagecoach United Counties 165 (9258 VC). It was originally registered N45 MJO with Thames Transit, who operated it on the Oxford Tube service.

Painted in Stagecoach corporate livery with Citybus fleet names, and seen here in its Hong Kong home, is Stagecoach Citybus Alexander-bodied tri-axle Volvo Olympian 510 (GW 1534). Originally registered GK 3258, it was new in May 1995 and was sold to Citybus in 1996 before returning to the Stagecoach fold when it purchased Citybus in March 1998. (Campbell Morrison)

New to Stagecoach Hong Kong with fleet number 7, Alexander-bodied tri-axle Volvo Olympian 506 (GK 2009) is seen here in Citybus livery shortly after the company was purchased by Stagecoach in March 1998. (Author's collection)

Stagecoach USA-owned Suburban Transit's MCI tri-axle 102C3 8020 (AC-698H) awaits its passengers while on a charter duty in New York in March 1999.

Heading through New York (USA) while undertaking a sightseeing tour in March 1999 is Stagecoach-owned Gray Line's ECW-bodied Bristol VRT D210 (BE 3989), which was new in the UK to West Yorkshire Road Car Co., with whom it was registered SWW 306R.

Seen at Battery Park, New York, while being operated by Stagecoach subsidiary Grayline Air Shuttle, open-top ECW-bodied Bristol VRT D216 began life in the UK, registered as TWR 468W with West Riding Automobile Company.

With a full load of passengers, Stagecoach Gray Line D236, a tri-axle open-top Neoplan, rushes past the now sadly destroyed World Trade Centre in March 1999.

Standing in the yard of Stagecoach Transit's Stockton-on-Tees depot on 24 November 1999, having just arrived from Stagecoach East London, is Alexander-bodied Dennis Dart DAL3 (N303 AMC).

Freshly repainted, Stagecoach Cheltenham & Gloucester Leyland National 3062 (TAE 644S) stands outside Cheltenham depot on 13 April 1997.

Fitted with a new electronic destination screen, Stagecoach Coastline Buses ex-East London Leyland Titan 7221 (OHV 761Y) passes Coastline's Northern Counties-bodied Volvo Olympian 244 (L244 SDY) in Portsmouth in 1999. (F. W. York)